Are You
Satisfied
with Jesus?

Andrew Wommack

ISBN 978-1-59548-443-7

Published by Andrew Wommack Ministries, Inc.
Woodland Park, CO 80863
awmi.net

For Worldwide Distribution, Printed in the USA

2 3 4 5 6 / 26 25 24 23

Contents

The night before Jesus' crucifixion, He told His disciples that they knew where He was going and how to get there. Thomas disagreed with Him by saying they didn't know where He was going, and therefore, they couldn't know the way. Jesus responded by saying,

> *I am the way, the truth, and the life: no man cometh unto the Father, but by me.*

John 14:6

He went on to say that if they had really known Him, they would have known the Father also, because seeing Him was seeing the Father. Philip responded, "Show us the Father and it will satisfy us" (see John 14:8).

Philip's statement deserves closer examination.

Philip wasn't completely satisfied with Jesus. Although he had witnessed Jesus perform miracles that no one had ever done before, speak as no one had ever spoken before, and love him as no one had ever loved him before, that wasn't enough. He wanted something more than Jesus before he would be satisfied.

According to the *Oxford Dictionary*, the word *satisfy* means, "meet the expectations, needs, or desires of (someone); fulfill (a desire or need); provide (someone) with adequate information or proof so they are convinced about something." Think about that. In Philip's estimation, Jesus hadn't fulfilled all of Philip's expectations. He hadn't met his desires. He hadn't provided Philip with adequate proof. Philip was wanting more than Jesus.

Wow! If Jesus doesn't satisfy you, who or what will?

Are you satisfied with Jesus? Do you have expectations, needs, or desires beyond what Jesus has provided? Do you need more information or proof beyond what Jesus has provided you?

Why Wasn't Philip Satisfied with Jesus?

It was because Philip only knew Jesus according to His flesh (2 Cor. 5:16). That is to say, Philip didn't know the real Jesus. He didn't fully recognize who Jesus was because of His physical body. Jesus' humanity hid His divinity from them.

Jesus was God manifest in the flesh (1 Tim. 3:16). Jesus was the Lord God Almighty at His birth (Luke 2:11), but that glory was wrapped in the physical flesh of a tiny baby. His flesh was sinless, but it was still flesh. Isaiah said that there was no beauty in Jesus' flesh that He should be desired

(Is. 53:2). Jesus had to grow in His physical body and in His physical mind (Luke 2:52). His flesh looked as natural as any ordinary man.

And because the true person of Jesus was veiled by His flesh, Philip and the other disciples didn't fully recognize who Jesus really was. They had the disadvantage of seeing Jesus' physical body.

> "For unto you is born this day in the city of David a Saviour, which is Christ the Lord."
> — Luke 2:11

Maybe you're thinking, *What do you mean 'disadvantage?' It would have been wonderful to be one of Jesus' twelve disciples and see Him in the flesh!* Yes, it would have, but it would also have made it harder to perceive who Jesus really was.

They saw Jesus in all of His humanity. He got tired, hungry, and dirty. He had to eat, sleep, and do all the things we have to do. It would have been hard to look at the humanity of Jesus and think, *This is God! This is the One who created the heavens and the earth* (Gen. 1:1). *This is the One who can fit the whole universe in the palm of His right hand* (Is. 48:13), *yet He's just like me.*

I once had a dream where I was one of Jesus' disciples. It was so vivid, I thought it was real. I saw Him raise the dead and give sight to the blind. I was rejoicing with the other disciples over all the things we had seen and heard. Then Jesus turned around and challenged me by saying, "But who do you say I am?" Although I had seen Him do things that no mortal man could do, when I looked straight into the face of his humanity, it took all the faith I could muster to say, "You are the Christ, the Son of the living God" (see Matt. 16:15–16). I had to go beyond what I was seeing

> "In the beginning God created the heaven and the earth."
> – Genesis 1:1

with my eyes, and I had to speak from my heart by faith (Rom. 10:10). Through that dream, I can somewhat imagine how hard it must have been for the disciples.

We have the advantage of seeing Jesus through the scriptures with the witness of the indwelling Holy Spirit. Jesus' twelve disciples had to overcome Jesus' humanity every day. We don't. They only knew Jesus after the flesh (2 Cor. 5:16). We can see Jesus with the eyes of our hearts through the revelation God has given us in Scripture. They couldn't do that.

> "Thou art the Christ, the Son of the living God."
> — Matthew 16:16

Jesus went on to ask Philip a question. In John 14:9, He said,

Have I been so long time with you, and yet hast thou not known me, Philip? he that hath seen me hath seen the Father; and how

sayest thou then, Shew us the Father?

Jesus was saying that if Philip had known Him, the real Him, he would have known the Father. Seeing who Jesus really was on the inside was the exact same thing as seeing the Father. He wasn't speaking about seeing His physical body. Our Lord was saying that if they had seen His heart, they would have seen the heart of God. Jesus and His Father are One, and Jesus is the perfect representation of His Father God (Heb. 1:3).

That's exactly what Paul was referring to in 2 Corinthians 5:16, which says, *"though we have known Christ after the flesh, yet now henceforth know we him no more."* When he said he had known Jesus after the flesh, Paul was referring to being a student of Gamaliel and living in Jerusalem (Acts 22:3). Certainly, he had seen Jesus many times during His ministry in Jerusalem. He could have recognized Jesus and described his physical features. But

Paul obviously missed who Jesus really was until his encounter with the resurrected Jesus on the road to Damascus (Acts 9). After that, Paul *knew* Jesus in a way that went far beyond

> Our Lord was saying that if they had seen His heart, they would have seen the heart of God.

just the physical. It is only through the Spirit that we can truly know who Jesus really is (1 Cor. 2:14).

Jesus in Another Form

There are eight recorded instances of Jesus appearing to His disciples after His resurrection, and in nearly every case they had trouble recognizing Him. In Mark 16:9, Mary Magdalene thought Jesus was the gardener until she recognized Him by the way He called her name. The two disciples on the way to Emmaus spent over an hour talking with Jesus, and yet didn't recognize Him by sight.

It wasn't until Jesus blessed the meal, as He had done at the Last Supper, that their spiritual eyes were opened and they knew Him (Luke 24:13–31). Later that same resurrection day, Jesus had to show the scars in His hands to prove to His disciples that it was really Him (Luke 24:36–39).

> "But the natural man receiveth not the things of the Spirit of God: for they are foolishness unto him: neither can he know *them*, because they are spiritually discerned."
> – 1 Corinthians 2:14

When Jesus was eating with some of the twelve at the Sea of Galilee, John 21:12 says,

And none of the disciples durst ask him, Who art thou? knowing that it was the Lord.

Why would they even have the desire to ask Him who He was if they recognized Him? It should have been obvious, but yet they thought about asking that question because they didn't recognize Him by sight.

The clearest example of their inability to recognize Jesus is recorded in Matthew 28:16–17, which says, *"Then the eleven disciples went away into Galilee, into a mountain where Jesus had appointed them. And when they saw him, they worshipped him: but some doubted."* These were the remaining eleven disciples who had spent the last three and a half years with Jesus every day and night. They were looking at Him face to face, and yet some of them doubted this was really Jesus. *What was going on? Why did those who knew Jesus intimately have trouble recognizing Him?*

The answer lies in 1 Corinthians 2:14. That verse says,

> *But the natural man receiveth not the things of the Spirit of God: for they are foolishness*

unto him: neither can he know them, *because they are spiritually discerned.*

The resurrected Jesus was in His glorified body, which was not just physical anymore.

There was a physical aspect to it because Jesus said He had flesh and bones (Luke 24:39). But Jesus' resurrected body wasn't only natural anymore. He could pass through locked doors (John 20:19) and appear and disappear (Luke 24:31). He now had to be spiritually discerned, and the disciples weren't spiritual.

They had only known Jesus through their five senses, not their spirits. Now that Jesus was in His glorified body, they didn't recognize Him because He had to be spiritually discerned. The instance recorded in Luke 24 about the two disciples who walked with Jesus for over an hour and yet didn't recognize Him, was summed up by one verse, Mark 16:12, that says,

After that he appeared in another form unto two of them, as they walked, and went into the country.

The "another form" mentioned isn't saying He didn't look human or looked like another human. It was speaking of Jesus being in His glorified body. He still had the print of the nails in His hands and feet (Luke 24:39) and the scar from the spear in His side (John 20:20).

It's possible that His face bore scars that might have affected His appearance, which in itself is amazing. When we are resurrected, our bodies will be restored perfectly without defect, but our Savior's resurrected body will still bear the scars of His crucifixion. The only resurrected body in heaven that will have scars from this earth life will be that of Jesus. What love that He would forever want to be reminded of the price He paid for us.

It was the fact that Jesus was now spiritual, and the disciples were carnal, which blinded them to who He was. They had known Jesus through the flesh during His earthly ministry, but after the resurrection they had to know Him by the spirit. They weren't born again yet and didn't have that ability.

The apostle John leaned on Jesus' chest as they reclined at the Last Supper (John 13:23). This was totally appropriate, but John could only do that because Jesus' flesh concealed His true glory. When John saw Jesus on the Isle of Patmos in all His glory, the same John who had leaned on his chest at the last supper now fell at His feet as if he were dead (Rev. 1:17). Jesus was the same in spirit during the Last Supper as He was when He appeared to John on the Isle of Patmos, but now that natural flesh had been replaced by His glorified spiritual body.

So, going back to Philip's statement that he wouldn't be satisfied until He saw the Father; the problem wasn't that Jesus wasn't enough to satisfy. The problem was that Philip didn't look past Jesus' flesh to see who Jesus was in the spirit.

God is a spirit (John 4:24) and Jesus was totally God in His spirit, although He was robed in a sinless physical body.

They had known Jesus through the flesh during His earthly ministry but after the resurrection they had to know Him by the spirit.

Philip was only using his five senses, and he could only perceive things in the physical realm. He missed the real treasure of who Jesus was in the spirit because he was dominated by what he saw and felt. That blinded Philip to who Jesus really was.

Our flesh is comparable to the vehicle we drive. It enables us to get around in this world. Many people know me by the pickup I drive. They see my pickup go by and they say, "There goes Andrew." But that's not the real me.

If I drove up to their house and they came out and hugged my pickup, or talked to my pickup, that would be weird. It is just the vehicle I get around in. The real me is inside.

Likewise, Jesus' body was just the vehicle that allowed him to get around while in this world. If we had been God and decided to become a man, we would have chosen a stretch limousine as our vehicle, but Jesus chose a plain ol' car that blended in with everyone else.

He missed the real treasure of who Jesus was in the spirit because he was dominated by what he saw and felt.

Isaiah 53:2 says that when we see Him, there is no beauty that we should desire Him. Jesus' flesh was sinless but ordinary in every way that ours is. In that sense, it was like a veil that shielded people from seeing the real Jesus that was inside.

If you understand this, then it opens up a whole new realm of understanding about our relationship with the Lord.

A New Way to Know

Through the scriptures, we can know Jesus in a way that His own disciples couldn't until their new birth. The Holy Spirit reveals Jesus in all of His glory to us through the Bible. The Word of God is alive and powerful (Heb. 4:12) because it is Jesus.

In the beginning was the Word and the Word was with God and the Word was God.

John 1:1

When Jesus came into this earth, *"The Word was made flesh, and dwelt among us..."* (John 1:14). Jesus and the Word are One in the same way that Jesus and His Father are One.

Knowing Jesus through the Word of God is the same as knowing the Father through Jesus. If the disciples had known the true Jesus, they would have known God. Those who know the true Word of God by the revelation of the Holy Spirit know the true Jesus. And that should satisfy us. But sadly, all of us are more dominated by our flesh (senses) than we should be. We still try to connect with Jesus through our senses instead of through faith in the revealed Word of God.

Let me illustrate that through the way most Christians perceive the love of God.

Jesus said,

But whosoever drinketh of the water that I shall give him shall never thirst; but the water that I shall give him shall be in him a well of water springing up into everlasting life."

John 4:14

Jesus said in John 7:37–38,

If any man thirst, let him come unto me, and drink. He that believeth on me, as the scripture hath said, out of his belly shall flow rivers of living water.

These statements by Jesus make it crystal clear that once we drink of the water of life we will never thirst again. It will be like an artesian well where the life-giving water doesn't have to be pumped out but springs up constantly. Yet that's not what most Christians experience.

The average Christian is longing to experience the love of God in some emotional way instead of enjoying what we already have in the spirit. God commended His love to us while we were yet sinners, and He loves us

> Knowing Jesus through the Word of God is the same as knowing the Father through Jesus.

even more now (Rom. 5:8–9). Galatians 5:22–23 says,

> *But the fruit of the Spirit is love, joy, peace, longsuffering, gentleness, goodness, faith, Meekness, temperance: against such there is no law.*

This fruit isn't produced seasonally. It's constant. We always have God's love, joy, and peace in our spirits. The problem with us is the same as Philip's problem. We are looking to connect with the Lord in the wrong way—through our senses instead of our new, born-again spirits.

Walking in the Flesh

This is what the Bible calls walking in the flesh instead of walking in the spirit (Gal. 5:16). Those that are in the flesh cannot please God (Rom. 8:8). Jesus said in John 3:6,

That which is born of the flesh is flesh; and that which is born of the Spirit is spirit.

Today we would say, "Flesh is flesh, and Spirit is spirit." They are two different realms, and to truly worship God, we have to connect with Him in and through our spirit (John 4:24).

There have been many Christian songs that glorify being hungry and thirsty for the Lord to the point of desperation. How does that fit with Jesus' statements that we would never thirst again? It doesn't. Those songs are describing people who are longing for God in their flesh.

> The average Christian is longing to experience the love of God in some emotional way instead of enjoying what we already have in the spirit.

They want Him to do something that will go beyond the spiritual and manifest something in the physical, so they won't have to walk by faith. Is it possible that when we are magnifying our dissatisfaction in the physical, we are acting like Philip and missing what is reality in the spirit?

Still you might say, "But I'm not satisfied. I'm discouraged. I'm depressed. I'm fearful." And on and on the descriptions could go. You might not realize it, but you are making the same mistake Philip made. You are only doing an inventory on what you have in the natural. In your spirit, you are complete (Col. 2:9–10).

Philip was judging only by the natural realm. He wasn't aware of who Jesus was in the spirit. Likewise, when we focus on our feelings, we are living only in the carnal realm. In the spirit, we have all of the fruit of the Spirit listed in Galatians 5:22: *"love, joy, peace,"* etc.

Just as Jesus was everything the disciples could have ever wanted but they didn't perceive, so in our born-again spirits we have everything we will ever need or could ever want. We are identical to Jesus right now in our spirit (1 John 4:17; 1 Cor. 6:17). We just aren't perceiving it.

We have to go beyond our feelings and emotions and begin to walk in the spirit. Jesus said in John 6:63,

> **In your spirit you are complete.**

It is the spirit that quickeneth; the flesh profiteth nothing: the words that I speak unto you, they *are spirit, and* they *are life.*

When we walk in the truths of God's Word, we are walking in the spirit. When we go by how we feel, we are walking after the flesh. And remember that you can't know Jesus after the flesh anymore (2 Cor. 5:16).

Some of the last words of Jesus before He ascended back into heaven were *"Lo, I am with you*

alway, even unto the end of the world" (Matt. 28:20).
The writer of Hebrews quoted Jesus as saying, *"I will never leave thee, nor forsake thee"* (Heb. 13:5). This leaves no doubt that Jesus is always with us whether we feel it or not. But we often are more impacted by our feelings than what God's Word says. We beg the Lord to be with us when we meet in church despite the fact He has already promised us that where two or three are gathered in His name, there He is in the midst of us (Matt. 18:20). We ask Him to go with us as we leave church, which is directly against his promise of being with us always. We go by what we feel and see instead of the revelation of His Word.

> We have to go beyond our feelings and emotions and begin to walk in the spirit.

That's like Philip saying he wasn't satisfied with Jesus, but he would be satisfied if he could see the Father. We say, "I know the Word promises He is

23

> This leaves no doubt that Jesus is always with us whether we feel it or not.

always with me, but I don't feel it. I want to feel something." Philip was in the very presence of the Father by being in Jesus' presence, but he missed it because he was going by sight and feelings. Likewise, Jesus is always with us, but we often are more controlled by what we feel than what we believe.

Truly with You

I had a miraculous encounter with the Lord on March 23, 1968. I was caught up in the presence and love of God for over four months. I could feel His love and acceptance. It was awesome! But the feeling didn't last, and desperation set in. I got drafted in 1969 and sent to Vietnam. While in Vietnam, I was desperate to get that feeling of God's love and presence back.

I was fasting and praying and begging God for another encounter. Then one day, it was like God left me. All sensitivity to God and any awareness of Him left. I panicked. I literally hid in a little closet in my bunker and covered myself with clothes so I wouldn't have to talk to anyone. I was paralyzed by fear. I would have given anything to just get back to the way it was.

This went on for three days. On the fourth morning, I woke up kneeling next to my cot praying, and things went back to normal. There wasn't anything special. I didn't have another encounter where I was caught up in the love of God. There were no bells and whistles, or angelic visitations. I was just back to "normal." I once again had the peace of knowing that the Lord was with me whether I felt it or not.

I now know that the Lord never left me (Heb. 13:5), but I think He got tired of hearing me gripe and complain and beg for some special epiphany, where I could just go by my feelings and not walk by faith (2 Cor. 5:7). Therefore, He showed me what it would feel like to be totally without Him. It was terrible. I think that is what hell will be like. There will be no God and nothing good in hell. That's as close to hell as I ever want to come.

I learned from that experience that God was always with me whether I have an emotional experience or not. Since that day, I have not asked for some special touch or proof of His presence. I am satisfied. I believe He is always with me because of what God's Word says. I don't have to feel it.

Yes, He Loves You

Are you satisfied, or are you looking for something more to assure you that God loves you?

I have people come up to me often and ask me to pray that the Lord will pour His love out in their life. To their amazement, I won't pray a prayer like that. They are shocked and ask, "Why? Isn't it godly to ask for God's love?" Nope! That is inferring that God's Word isn't true.

> I believe He is always with me because of what God's Word says. I don't have to feel it.

The Bible says in Romans 5:5,

And hope maketh not ashamed; because thelove of God is shed abroad in our hearts by the Holy Ghost which is given unto us.

Romans 5:8–10 says,

But God commendeth his love toward us, in that, while we were yet sinners, Christ died for us. Much more then, being now justified by his blood, we shall be saved from wrath through him. For if, when we were enemies, we were reconciled to God by the death of his Son, much more, being reconciled, we shall be saved by his life.

This love is now a fruit of the Spirit that indwells us (Gal. 5:22). God has never and will never take back His love for us. Therefore, if we aren't feeling God's love, our feelings are wrong. God loves you whether you feel it or not. We need to go by the truth revealed in God's Word and not our feelings.

In our modern culture, feelings have been exalted to a position God never intended them to occupy. Ephesians 4:19 says,

Who being past feeling have given themselves over unto lasciviousness, to work all uncleanness with greediness.

This is describing going beyond the proper use of our feelings and being completely given over to sensuality, where feelings trump fact. That pretty much sums up most people's lives today.

People will say, "Nobody loves me." They know that's not true. Somebody loves them. Certainly, God loves them, but they don't feel it. It doesn't matter what God's Word says because something negative has happened to capture their attention, and they have given themselves over to those feel-

> God loves you whether you feel it or not.

ings. They don't feel His love, so they come and ask me to have the Lord to do something to show them He loves them.

I won't dignify their feelings and insult the Lord by asking Him to do something that He has already done. That would be similar to Philip saying, "Show us the Father, and we will be satisfied" (see John 14:8). They are only satisfied when their flesh experiences it—when something happens to allow their five senses to perceive it. That's what the Bible calls *carnal*.

What Controls You?

To most people, the word *carnal* is describing something very sinful. They think murderers and rapists are carnal. That's absolutely true, but carnality isn't limited to only very sinful acts. When the Bible uses the word *carnal*, it is describing being controlled by your senses.

All sin is carnal, but not all carnality is sin. A person who is letting their emotions control them is carnal; that was Philip's problem—and all too often, our problem too.

I once had a student who counseled a young girl who felt her parents were oppressive and totally unfair in their treatment of her. The lady who was counseling her knew the girl's parents very well and knew that wasn't true. They weren't perfect parents. None are. But they loved her and were pointing her in the right direction. This girl had interpreted their demand that she go to church and live a godly life as child abuse.

> When the Bible uses the word carnal it is describing being controlled by your senses.

But our student counselor said, "It didn't matter what the truth was. To this girl, it was true. That's all that mattered." So, she went ahead and counseled her on how to forgive her parents as if they were the problem. I think that's terrible. I hate that.

That is reinforcing the problem instead of dealing with it. Truth trumps feelings in God's kingdom. And when we are more controlled by our feelings than by the truth of Scripture, then we aren't satisfied with Jesus (the Word), just like Philip. This girl should have been made

> All sin is carnal, but not all carnality is sin.

to see the truth and get her emotions in line with God's Word. But very few people let the Bible get in the way of what they feel.

Those who promote feelings over truth will go through life with a chip on their shoulder that Satan will be more than glad to knock off every single day. There will always be some problem, or the potential for a problem, in our life. If we are waiting until all problems are removed and everything is perfect before we feel God's love, we will never have love, joy, and peace. Those things are already present in our spirit. We just need to walk in the spirit instead of in the flesh.

A New Creation

When I got back from Vietnam, I was pondering all of these things and trying to understand 2 Corinthians 5:17. That verse says,

Therefore if any man be in Christ, he is a new creature: old things are passed away; behold, all things are become new.

Suddenly the light came on, and I received one of the greatest revelations of my life.

I understood that the part of me that was saved was not my body or my emotions, but my spirit. That was easily discerned by examination. My body hadn't passed away and all things become new. I have a promise of that happening (1 Cor. 15:51–55), but it hasn't happened yet. And my mind and emotions

> Very few people let the Bible get in the way of what they feel.

haven't changed. Paul said in 1 Corinthians 13:12 that we don't see everything clearly now, but in eternity we will know everything, even as we are known. That certainly hasn't happened yet.

So, that only leaves my spirit as the part that was changed (1 Thess. 5:23). My spirit is where all of my salvation is deposited. I can draw out that life through the renewing of my mind, but it doesn't happen automatically. My life goes in the direction of my dominant thoughts (Prov. 23:7).

If I continue to use only my five senses (what I can see, taste, hear, smell, and feel), then I will experience the death that comes from thinking like everyone else (Rom. 8:6). But if

> **Suddenly the light came on and I received one of the greatest revelations of my life.**

I renew my mind to the truths of what has happened to my born-again spirit, I will find the good, acceptable, and perfect will of God (Rom.12:2).

I have found my satisfaction with what Jesus has already done and who I already am in my born-again spirit. That spirit is complete. It's not in the process of growing or acquiring more of

God. My spirit is perfect and complete right now. One third of my salvation (the spirit) is over. It's as perfect and complete as it will ever be in heaven. When I get to heaven, my spirit will not have to be cleansed or injected with more of anything. As Jesus is, that's exactly the way I am in my spirit right now (1 John 4:17), because my born-again spirit is the spirit of Jesus sent into my heart (Gal. 4:6). If anyone doesn't have the Spirit of Christ living in them, then they are not true believers (Rom. 8:9). Therefore, all who are truly saved already have the fulness of God in them right now (John 1:16), whether they feel it or not.

This has revolutionized my life. I no longer look at things through these physical eyes only. I now look with my heart through the revelation of God's Word, and everything looks different. I'm not trying to get God to love me. He has already proven that to me without a doubt. There are times that life distracts me and gets my attention on other things, and the emotion of that isn't as strong as other times. But when I realize that, I simply get back in the spirit (John 6:63) and focus my attention on what God has already

> Therefore, all who are truly saved already have the fulness of God in them right now (John 1:16), whether they feel it or not.

done. I don't ask for more, but I draw on what has already been given to me. Praise the Lord!

Receive Jesus as Your Savior

Choosing to receive Jesus Christ as your Lord and Savior is the most important decision you'll ever make!

God's Word promises, *"That if thou shalt confess with thy mouth the Lord Jesus, and shalt believe in thine heart that God hath raised him from the dead, thou shalt be saved. For with the heart man believeth unto righteousness; and with the mouth confession is made unto salvation"* (Rom. 10:9–10). *"For whosoever shall call upon the name of the Lord shall be saved"* (Rom. 10:13). By His grace, God has already done everything to provide salvation. Your part is simply to believe and receive.

Pray out loud: "Jesus, I acknowledge that I've sinned and need to receive what you did for the forgiveness of my sins. I confess that You are my Lord and Savior. I believe in my heart that God raised You from the dead. By faith in Your Word, I receive salvation now. Thank You for saving me."

The very moment you commit your life to Jesus Christ, the truth of His Word instantly comes to pass in your spirit. Now that you're born again, there's a brand-new you!

Please contact us and let us know that you've prayed to receive Jesus as your Savior. We'd like to send you some free materials to help you on your new journey. Call our Helpline: **719-635-1111** (available 24 hours a day, seven days a week) to speak to a staff member who is here to help you understand and grow in your new relationship with the Lord.

Welcome to your new life!

Receive the Holy Spirit

As His child, your loving heavenly Father wants to give you the supernatural power you need to live a new life. *"For every one that asketh receiveth; and he that seeketh findeth; and to him that knocketh it shall be opened...how much more shall your heavenly Father give the Holy Spirit to them that ask him?"* (Luke 11:10–13).

All you have to do is ask, believe, and receive! Pray this: "Father, I recognize my need for Your power to live a new life. Please fill me with Your Holy Spirit. By faith, I receive it right now. Thank You for baptizing me. Holy Spirit, You are welcome in my life."

Some syllables from a language you don't recognize will rise up from your heart to your mouth (1 Cor. 14:14). As you speak them out loud by faith, you're releasing God's power from within and building yourself up in the spirit (1 Cor. 14:4). You can do this whenever and wherever you like.

It doesn't really matter whether you felt anything or not when you prayed to receive the Lord and His Spirit. If you believed in your heart that you received, then God's Word promises you did. *"Therefore I say unto you, What things soever ye desire, when ye pray, believe that ye receive* them, *and ye shall have* them"* (Mark 11:24). God always honors His Word—believe it!

We would like to rejoice with you, pray with you, and answer any questions to help you understand more fully what has taken place in your life!

Please contact us to let us know that you've prayed to be filled with the Holy Spirit and to request the book *The New You & the Holy Spirit*. This book will explain in more detail about the benefits of being filled with the Holy Spirit and speaking in tongues. Call our Helpline: **719-635-1111** (available 24 hours a day, seven days a week).

Call for Prayer

If you need prayer for any reason, you can call our Helpline, 24 hours a day, seven days a week at **719-635-1111**. A trained prayer minister will answer your call and pray with you.

Every day, we receive testimonies of healings and other miracles from our Helpline, and we are ministering God's nearly-too-good-to-be-true message of the Gospel to more people than ever. So, I encourage you to call today!

About the Author

Andrew Wommack's life was forever changed the moment he encountered the supernatural love of God on March 23, 1968. As a renowned Bible teacher and author, Andrew has made it his mission to change the way the world sees God.

Andrew's vision is to go as far and deep with the Gospel as possible. His message goes far through the *Gospel Truth* television program, which is available to over half the world's population. The message goes deep through discipleship at Charis Bible College, headquartered in Woodland Park, Colorado. Founded in 1994, Charis has campuses across the United States and around the globe.

Andrew also has an extensive library of teaching materials in print, audio, and video. More than 200,000 hours of free teachings can be accessed at **awmi.net**.

Contact Information

Andrew Wommack Ministries, Inc.
PO Box 3333
Colorado Springs, CO 80934-3333
info@awmi.net
awmi.net

Helpline: 719-635-1111 (available 24/7)

Charis Bible College
info@charisbiblecollege.org
844-360-9577
CharisBibleCollege.org

For a complete list of all of our offices,
visit **awmi.net/contact-us**.
Connect with us on social media.

CHARIS
BIBLE COLLEGE

God has more for you.

Are you longing to find your God-given purpose? At Charis Bible College you will establish a firm foundation in the Word of God and receive hands-on ministry experience to **find, follow,** and **fulfill** your purpose.

Scan the QR code for a free Charis teaching!

CharisBibleCollege.org
Admissions@awmcharis.com
(844) 360-9577

Change your life. **Change the world.**